Everything I Know I Learned Over Tea

Emilie Barnes
with Anne Christian Buchanan

Paintings by Susan Rios

HARVEST HOUSE PUBLISHERS

EUGENE, OREGON

Everything I Know I Learned Over Tea

Text Copyright © 2004 by Harvest House Publishers
Published by Harvest House Publishers
Eugene, OR 97402

ISBN 0-7369-1390-4

For more information about Emilie Barnes, please send a self-addressed, stamped envelope to:
More Hours in My Day
2150 Whitestone Drive
Riverside, CA 92506
(909) 369-4093

Original Artwork © Susan Rios. Licensed by Art Impressions, Canoga Park, CA. For more information regarding artwork featured in this book, please contact Susan Rios, Inc., (818) 995-7467 or www.susanriosinc.com.

Design and production by Garborg Design Works, Minneapolis, Minnesota

Portions of this book are excerpted from *If Teacups Could Talk* (Harvest House Publishers, 1994), *The Twelve Teas of Friendship* (Harvest House Publishers, 2001), and *The Twelve Teas of Celebration* (Harvest House Publishers, 2003).

Verses are taken from the Holy Bible: New International Version®. NIV®. Copyright © 1973, 1978, 1984 by the International Bible Society. Used by permission of Zondervan Publishing House.

Printed in Hong Kong.

04 05 06 07 08 09 10 11 12 13 / NG / 10 9 8 7 6 5 4 3 2

Everything I Know I Learned Over Tea...

All it takes is an invitation.

The wonder of tea is the spirit of tea.

A whistling kettle is the prelude to a lovely conversation.

Everyone brings something special to the table.

Teacups are fragile...and resilient.

Two cups will warm two hearts.

A shared heirloom is more valuable.

Variety infuses tea with flavor.

Savor the beauty of a moment.

Tradition is a comfort.

Every occasion is a celebration.

For best results: Let tea steep.

Always say thank you.

All it takes is an invitation.

Find yourself a cup of tea,
the teapot is behind you.
Now tell me about
hundreds of things.

SAKI

If teacups could talk my house would be full of conversation...because my house is full of teacups.

Some of these cups I inherited from women I love— my mother and my aunties. Some are gifts from my husband, Bob, or from my children or from special friends. A few are delightful finds from elegant boutiques or dusty antiques shops.

One cup bears telltale cracks and scars; it was the only one I could salvage when a shelf slipped and fourteen cups fell in shatters.

Yet another cup, a gift, is of a style I've never much cared for, but now it makes me smile as I remember the houseguest who

5

"rescued" it from a dark corner of the armoire because it looked "lonely."

Each one of my teacups has a history, and each one is precious to me. I have gladly shared them with guests and told their stories to many people.

Recently, however, I have been more inclined to listen.

I've been wondering what all those cups, with their history and long experience, are trying to say to *me*.

What I hear from them, over and over, is an invitation—one I want to extend to you: *When did you last have a tea party? When was the last time you enjoyed a cup of tea with someone you care about? Isn't it time you did it again?*

Whether it is penned in calligraphy or offered as an afterthought on the phone...a heartfelt invitation is all it takes for something wonderful to happen.

"I can just imagine myself sitting down at the head of the table and pouring out the tea," said Anne, shutting her eyes ecstatically. "And asking Diana if she takes sugar! I know she doesn't but of course I'll ask her just as if I didn't know."

L.M. MONTGOMERY
Anne of Green Gables

Susan Rios '81

The wonder of tea is the spirit of tea.

The mug from the washstand was used as Becky's tea cup,
and the tea was so delicious that it was not necessary
to pretend that it was anything but tea.

FRANCES HODGSON BURNETT
A Little Princess

*P*erhaps the idea of a tea party takes you back to childhood. Do you remember dressing up and putting on your best manners as you sipped pretend tea out of tiny cups and shared pretend delicacies with your friends, your parents, or your teddy bears?

Does the mention of teatime bring quieter memories—a bit of chamomile sipped in solitude on a big porch, or friendly confidences shared over steaming cups? So many of my special times of closeness—with my husband, my children, my friends—have begun with putting a kettle on to boil and pulling out a tea tray.

Even if you prefer coffee, cocoa, or lemonade...or you like chunky mugs better than delicate china, a tea party prepared in the right spirit is all that matters.

You see, it's not tea itself that speaks to the soul with such a satisfying message. And it's not the teacups themselves that bring such a message of serenity and friendship.

The wonder of tea is what happens when women or men or children make a place in their life for the ritual of sharing. I have shared delightful tea moments with everyone, from business executives to book-club ladies to five-year-old boys.

When we bother with the little extras that feed the soul and nurture the senses and make space for unhurried conversations, what fills the cups is irrelevant.

After all, it is the spirit of the tea party that fills hearts to the brim with joy.

The "art of tea" is a spiritual force for us to share.
ALEXANDRA STODDARD

A whistling kettle is the prelude to a lovely conversation.

Somehow taking tea together encourages an atmosphere of intimacy when you slip off the timepiece in your mind and cast your fate to a delight of tasty tea, tiny foods, and thoughtful conversation.

GAIL GRECO

The very act of preparing and serving tea encourages conversation. The little spaces in time created by teatime rituals call out to be filled with conversation.

Teatime supports a conversation by giving us something to do when the dialogue lags...or hits an uncomfortable snag. If we don't know what to say, we can always pick up another muffin or freshen our companion's cup or just inhale the aroma of our own cup, and thus negotiate the silences to explore deeper levels of companionship.

The relative formality of a traditional teatime also imposes a kind of gentle control on the confidences we share. Teatime is intimate but not intrusive—it feels so safe, so nurturing. It fosters civilized friendship, and in this age of chaos a sense of safety is rare and comforting.

11

The calmness of tea is ideal for getting to know someone new, for patching up a misunderstanding, for sharing good news, or supporting one another in bad times. I have seen lives change over teacups.

There is a great deal of poetry and fine sentiment in a chest of tea.

RALPH WALDO EMERSON

That's why I want to treat my teatime companions—strangers, friends, or family—with the same gentleness and respect I reserve for the delicate china teacups. That's why I want to be fully present—in heart, soul, and mind—to enjoy the sweet communion of kindred spirits over a cup of tea.

The Art of Conversation

To blend new friends and old, inspire engaging conversation with these starter questions.

- Where did your family live when you were six? When you were twelve?
- What is the most valuable thing you've learned in the past ten years?
- What is the most encouraging word anyone can say to you?
- What is the greatest gift you have ever received?
- What's your idea of a truly perfect morning? What would you do?

13

Everyone brings something special to the table.

What better way to suggest friendliness—
and to create it—than with a cup of tea?

J. GRAYSON LUTTRELL

One Saturday afternoon my ten-year-old granddaughter Christine said, "Grammy, let's make some scones and have some tea." So we did.

And I am so glad, because once the tea was poured, we began to talk—about friendships, family, and what she could expect as a preadolescent. I was amazed at her maturity. We even talked about spiritual matters—about God and the meaning of life.

We were forty-five years apart in age, yet seconds apart in spirit.

It was only afterward, as I was carefully washing the china cups, that I realized what really had happened: Christine had asked for a tea party, but what she was really asking for was *time with me.*

Tea nurtures friendship by inviting us to

be present to one another—right now, in the moment.

So much in our culture can be done without really being there—without being mentally and emotionally tuned in to the people around us or the task at hand. We can go to entertainment events or even to church and sit side by side without truly connecting with one another.

And when we offer tea to someone, we are also offering ourselves. We are saying, "For the next few minutes I will listen to you. I will treat you with respect. I will be present for you."

A Loving Recipe for a Perfect Cup of Tea

1 willing friend who loves to sit and share
1 grateful heart to have a friend that cares
1 beautiful garden to show us God is near
Many wonderful memories of times shared throughout the years
Lots of smiles and laughter to brighten up our days
Many prayers that we prayed for each other along the way

AUTHOR UNKNOWN

Teacups are fragile...and resilient.

What part of confidante has that poor teapot played ever since the kindly plant was introduced among us. Why myriads of women have cried over it, to be sure!...Nature meant very kindly...when she made the tea plant; and with a little thought, what series of pictures and groups the fancy may conjure up and assemble round the teapot and cup.

WILLIAM MAKEPEACE THACKERAY

I learned something wonderful about teacups while watching a program on archaeology—ceramic objects may be breakable, but they are also amazingly resistant to weathering and corrosion and age. Much of what we know about ancient civilizations we have learned from bits of pottery they left behind. China dishes recovered from shipwrecks are often good as new, long after the ship itself has dissolved in the saltwater!

In other words, porcelain is fragile, but it's also remarkably durable.

Like life.

Like us.

Humans are beautiful and breakable, like china cups...yet we are also strong and resilient. And unlike my cups, humans can heal and grow and move beyond disaster. We can reach out to one another in courage and comfort.

So what will I do if or when disaster strikes?

I'll do what other resilient humans do—

I'll pick up the pieces.

I'll try to help someone and accept help if I need it.

And then, somehow, I'll have another cup of tea.

While there's tea, there's hope.

Sir Arthur Pinero

20

Flavors to Fill that Cup

What's your favorite cup o' tea?

Black teas—made from leaves that are allowed to "ferment" or oxidize, then are "fired" or heated to remove most of the moisture. The heat is what turns the leaves black. Black teas produce a hearty brew that is higher in caffeine content than other teas (but still lower than coffee).

Green teas—are not fermented. Instead, the leaves are steamed in large vats before being fired. Green teas are delicate in flavor, light in color, low in caffeine, and very soothing—good for settling the stomach. They are usually enjoyed without sugar, cream, or lemon.

Oolong teas—produced by a relatively new process. Partially fermented with a taste that is stronger than green tea, more delicate than black tea.

Herbal teas—are not teas at all, but "infusions" from the leaves, roots, seeds, or fruits of various plants such as peppermint, jasmine, or chamomile. Herb teas are usually decaffeinated, and some have medicinal uses.

Two cups will warm two hearts.

What is the most wonderful thing for people like myself who follow the Way of Tea? My answer: the oneness of host and guest created through "meeting heart to heart" and sharing a bowl of tea.

SOSHITSU SEN
GRAND MASTER XIV
Urasenke School of Tea

It's one of the most important lessons we learn in life: We should always take care of the things we love. It is true of our treasured heirlooms just as it is true of our treasured friendships. If we want them to last, we need to invest some time and energy and thought into nurturing and maintaining them.

What keeps friendships alive and well? Spending time together and enjoying each other's company is a way to nurture those relationships of importance. One must take time for the preparation of tea in order to enjoy the

pleasures of tea. Friendship is exactly the same. Even if you live miles away from a special person, you can stay close with letters, emails, phone calls, and just by spending time in thought and prayer for another.

Preparing your heart for friendship allows those times when you are together to be rich, meaningful, warm, and flavorful.

Although my neighbors are all barbarians,
And you, you are a thousand miles away,
There are always two cups on my table.

TANG DYNASTY

24

How to Be a Good Friend over Tea.

Select teas and treats that she adores.

Decorate the table in colors and flowers that remind you of her.

Give your friend freedom to be herself at all times.

Make your friend's spiritual well-being a priority. Pray together in the stillness of teatime.

Give her your discretion. Be a trusting, listening ear and a shoulder to lean on.

Tell your friend what you like about her. Build her up as you serve her tea.

Let the tea party be a celebration of joy and laughter.

Treasure your past together. Refill her cup and talk about times you have shared.

And don't forget: When you are having a cup of tea alone, call your friend to say you are thinking of her.

A shared heirloom is more valuable.

For where your treasure is, there will your heart be also.

THE BOOK OF MATTHEW

Collecting teacups in Southern California is really an act of faith. As I write, the memory is still fresh of a major earthquake not far from where I live. Our home was safely south of the epicenter, and my tea things were safe, but friends and acquaintances experienced days of aftershocks that left all their breakable treasures in shards and shatters.

Everyday dangers put my cups at risk—the cat, the feather duster, my grandchildren, my own carelessness. I take a risk in using them, in letting others use them. But it's a risk I choose to take because it brings me joy.

In our daily lives, we take a risk just walking out the door in the morning.

But if we let that reality stop us from living, we've already lost!

A full life requires courage. And my teacups, in all their lovely vulnerability, remind me to avoid the temptation to fall back on "safe"

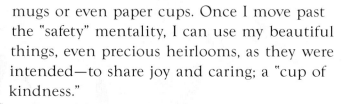

mugs or even paper cups. Once I move past the "safety" mentality, I can use my beautiful things, even precious heirlooms, as they were intended—to share joy and caring; a "cup of kindness."

Friendship involves risk and courage. Maybe there is someone you would like to get to know better. Perhaps a neighbor is going through a hard time, and you haven't had the courage to say more than "good morning." Maybe a friendship needs restoration.

Tea gives us a reason to step out, step up, and step into a new friendship. Do it. Our hearts, like teacups, become much more valuable when we use them to serve another.

I take a few quick sips. "This is really good." And I mean it. I have never tasted tea like this. It is smooth, pungent, and instantly addicting. "This is from Grand Auntie," my mother explains. "She told me 'If I buy the cheap tea, then I am saying that my whole life has not been worth something better.' A few years ago she bought it for herself. One hundred dollars a pound." "You're kidding." I take another sip. It tastes even better.

AMY TAN
The Kitchen God's Wife

Variety infuses tea with flavor.

There is the size of the leaf:
Its unique shape,
Its unique color,
Its unique fragrance,
A taste all its own,
And it changes...sip by sip.

RON RUBIN
Tea Things

Teatime offers so many wonderful possibilities for nurturing friendships. An inspired cup of tea represents an inspired life. I invite you to make full use of your creativity as you make the spirit of the tea party part of your life.

Think about your many friends, neighbors, and family

members. What is one thing that makes each person unique? Chances are as you run down the list you will think of many special qualities. Variety. It makes our life richer. It

Each cup of tea represents an imaginary voyage.
CATHERINE DOUZEL

gives our conversations depth and new direction. It awakens our spirit to the possibilities of life. It reminds us that we are all creative beings.

Add some variety to your life. It will make your cup so sweet.

The Spice of Life

Here is a gathering of unique tea-party ideas. Who would you invite to each of these teas?

Invite a friend to come for tea and bring along an unfinished craft project. After you enjoy your tea, play some soothing music, do your project, and talk.

For a sweet but different cup of tea, try adding a tablespoon of maple syrup to your cup. This would be a wonderful touch for an autumn tea—with decorations of colored leaves and bright apples.

Enliven any tea gathering by having each guest bring his or her teacup. You will learn so much about each other as you talk about your cups. Some will be from wedding sets, some family heirlooms, some hastily purchased for the occasion.

After a nap on a lazy afternoon, surprise your mate with a tea tray in bed.

Host an "adopt a grandma" or "adopt a kid" tea. Have everyone bring a guest who is over sixty—or under eight.

Build your tea around your favorite book that features tea. Some wonderful possibilities are: *Alice in Wonderland, Anne of Green Gables, Winnie-the-Pooh, Little Women*.

Plan your teas around the traditions of some of the great tea-drinking nations besides England—China, Japan, Israel, India, Russia, Scotland, Holland, or Ireland.

Gather a group of special friends to visit a local tea room or an inn that specializes in afternoon tea. This would be a wonderful reunion tradition: Gather each year at the tea room of your choice and reflect on the past year together.

Savor the beauty of a moment.

Never lose an opportunity of seeing anything that is beautiful; for beauty is God's handwriting—a wayside sacrament. Welcome it in every fair face, in every fair sky, in every fair flower, and thank God for it as a cup of blessing.

RALPH WALDO EMERSON

When I sit quietly on our patio in the morning with a cup of tea, I find I am much more acutely aware of the natural beauty around me—the swelling sunrise, the flowers blooming in their boxes by the door, the birds warming up their voices.

Teatime provides an environment of beauty as well. A traditional tea is above all a feast of loveliness, a delight to the senses.

Fingers delight in the cool smoothness of bone china, the warmth of steam rising from a cup, the contrasting textures of linen and lace, the coolness of a wafting breeze.

Noses tingle at the intoxicating mix of yeast and butter and cinnamon and roses.

Ears are soothed by lovely chamber music or warm conversation.

Eyes revel in the dainty symmetry of tea sandwiches prepared and

arranged, of sugar cubes in their bowl, of violets and ferns painted delicately on the gleaming teapot.

And all this happens before my taste buds begin to experience the sweet and savory delights that have been prepared.

Surely we have been given the gifts of creativity and sensitivity so we can grow more attuned to beauty, to the way things were meant to be.

You see, the most beautiful part of any tea party are the faces of friends...the sounds of their voices...the touch of their hands...and the fragrance of friendship mingling with the lovely aroma of tea. Don't miss a moment of such beauty.

The path to heaven passes through a teapot.

ANCIENT PROVERB

34

Susan Rios

Tradition is a comfort.

There are few hours in my life more agreeable than the hour dedicated to the ceremony known as afternoon tea.

HENRY JAMES

Tea was a tradition in my family when I was growing up. Because my family is Jewish, we enjoyed our tea in the tradition of Eastern European Jews. As I grew older, I discovered that the tradition of tea is included in many cultures and spans many centuries.

My first experience of afternoon tea in the traditional British style came during a trip to Canada, when my husband Bob and I visited the beautiful Empress Hotel in Victoria, British Columbia. I was enchanted by the experience and sought to learn more about this soul-satisfying custom. Now I enjoy my tea with fuller appreciation of its heritage.

Preparing and enjoying tea is a ritual in itself. It is a practice of tradition. Boiling the water in a kettle and arranging the tea tray is part of the ritual. My friend Yoli Brogger calls it "a ceremony of loveliness." I believe we all crave ceremony and loveliness.

When we do things a certain way, the way we have done them in the past, the way others before us have done them, something deep in our spirits is comforted.

Nowhere is the English genius of domesticity more notably evident than in the festival afternoon tea. The...chink of cups and the saucers tunes the mind to happy repose.

GEORGE GISSING

A satisfying aspect of a ritual lies in its repetition. The process for preparing tea is a moment of sweet repetition in our day. We can almost do it without thinking. So after a time, the ritual performs the valuable function of occupying the body and the senses while freeing the mind and spirit.

I enjoy my tea now with a sense of history, a sense of kinship with those who have gone before me. And somehow the brew seems all the richer.

Every occasion is a celebration.

"It's always tea-time..."

There is something about a tea party that brings out the best in people—the best behavior, the best intentions, the best attitudes. We expect a little more of each other when we come to tea, and we tend to live up to those expectations. We give a little more.

First of all, the traditional nature of the tea party says, "This is a special time." While teatime celebrations can be formal, they are also welcoming, personal, nonthreatening. Somehow sharing tea makes ordinary occasions seem special and special occasions seem comfortably ordinary.

Sipping tea across from others is not conducive to mindless revelry, but it is very supportive of conscious, deliberate joy. We think about what it is we're celebrating—the meaning of the occasion and the relationships of the people involved. Tea provides a gracious way to honor

40

accomplishments such as a new job, a graduation, a new marriage or baby. It adds a special touch to the observance of special days such as Mother's Day. The beautiful rituals speak the

If you are cold, tea will warm you;
If you are too heated, it will cool you;
If you are depressed, it will cheer you;
If you are exhausted, it will calm you.

WILLIAM GLADSTONE

unmistakable message of "I care" into the lives of others.

And best of all, tea can be a celebration in itself—an act of appreciation for the little everyday wonders that make up the texture of our lives. Rest in the moment and rejoice in simply being alive.

What Time Is Tea?

The hour...can be anywhere between three and six o'clock in the afternoon. The general rule is that the earlier tea is served, the lighter the refreshments. At three, tea is usually a snack—dainty finger sandwiches, petits fours, fresh strawberries; at six, it can be a meal—or "high" tea—with sausage rolls, salads, and trifle. You can serve high tea around the dining room table, but afternoon tea is more of a living room occasion, with everything brought in on a tray or a cart.

ANGELA HYNES
The Pleasures of Afternoon Tea

For best results: Let tea steep.

Tea! Thou soft, thou sober, sage and venerable liquid...
to whose glorious insipidity, I owe the happiest
moments of my life, let me fall prostrate.

COLLEY CIBBER

Have you ever noticed that your mind seems to work better when your body is occupied with something it's done before? This happens to me when I'm rinsing out a teapot or cutting the crust of sandwiches or arranging tea things on a tray. The repetitive actions of preparing and serving tea become a reassuring soil out of which thoughts can grow, and conversations can spring forth.

There's no hurry about any of this, since you can't go ahead with the tea until the water is boiling. And there's more waiting to do even then, because the tea leaves or teabags must steep in the pot. While you are waiting for the liquid to turn shades of

42

amber, carry the tray to a comfortable nook and wait in peace. If you are with friends, this is a wonderful time to reconnect. If you are alone, you can read, pray, or just "be."

When the cup is ready, and those first sips are savored, your mind will continue to relax; your words and your musings slow down and sift deeper. Your relationships—even your relationship with yourself—are granted space for a leisurely stretch.

All this slowness takes so little time. You may need to practice learning to enjoy the repetitive freedom of the ritual. But once you do, the blessings of time and comfort will infuse your soul with peace.

For if I could please myself I would always live as I lived there. I would choose always to breakfast at exactly eight and to be at my desk by nine, there to read or write till one. If a cup of good tea or coffee could be brought to me about eleven, so much the better.

C.S. LEWIS
Surprised by Joy

44

Brewing the Perfect Cup of Tea

Preparing a perfect cup of tea takes time. But these little steps can make the difference between a mediocre cup of tea and an excellent one.

1. Empty the teakettle and refill it with freshly drawn cold water. Put the kettle on to boil.
2. While the kettle is heating, pour hot water into the teapot to warm it. Ceramic (china, porcelain, stoneware) or glass teapots work best; tea brewed in a metal teapot may have a metallic taste.
3. Pour the hot water out of the teapot and add the tea. Measure a spoonful of loose tea for each cup desired into the warmed (empty) teapot, plus one extra spoonful for the pot. (Most teapots hold five to six cups.) If you are using teabags, use one bag less than the desired number of cups. Put the lid back on the pot until the water boils.
4. As soon as the kettle comes to a rolling boil, remove from heat. Overboiling causes the water to lose oxygen, and the resulting brew will taste flat.
5. Pour boiling water into the teapot and let the tea brew from three to six minutes. Small tea leaves will take less time to brew than large ones.
6. Gently stir the tea before pouring it through a tea strainer into the teacups. If you used teabags, remove them.

Always say thank you.

Cynthia came in quietly and set a cup of tea before him. He kissed her hand, inexpressibly grateful, and she went back into the kitchen. When we view the little things with thanksgiving, even they become big things.

JAN KARON
These High, Green Hills

There is something about a table set for tea that brings out the best manners in anyone. I have witnessed even the most wound-up children politely take their seats when called to tea. The social graces mothers try to instill in their children do emerge when a proper situation presents itself. Children of all ages treat the special ritual of teatime with reverence.

"Would you like some tea?"

"Yes, please."

"Would you like sugar?"

"Yes. Thank you very much."

Such simple exchanges embody the true spirit of the tea party. You see, serving tea is a peaceful moment of reciprocation. At a table covered in white lace and adorned with delicate cups, I learned to respect people.

I learned how to listen.

Share.

Offer.

Receive.

Tea presents an atmosphere where the give and take of a relationship—the ebb and flow of kindness and care—sets the rhythm for the moment.

And when I am alone, cozy in a chair with a blanket draped over my lap and a cup of tea on the side table, the same swell of gratitude fills me.

I take a moment to listen.

Share.

Offer.

Receive.

And most important of all...say thank you.